A Technology Q&A Book

Is That Robot Really My Doctor?

Photo credits:

AP Photo—Tsugufumi Matsumoto: p. 16; U.S. Department of Commerce: p. 22; HO: p. 25; Shizuo Kamabayashi: p. 25; U.S. Air Force, Senior Airman Michelle Leonard: p. 26
Electrolux—p. 13
FPG International—Gary Buss: pp. 9, 21; Ron Chapple: pp. 8, 27; Jim Cummins: p. 21; Jeffrey Sylvester: p. 9; Telegraph Colour Library: pp. 7, 15, 16; Arthur Tilley: p. 21; Tom Tracy: p. 24; VCG: p. 20
Illinois Institute of Technology—Bruce Quist: p. 29
International Stock—Richard Pharaoh: p. 11; Mike Agliolo: p. 20; Philip Wallick: p. 27
Lawrence Livermore National Laboratory—p. 29
Maglev, Inc.—p. 22
Microsoft—p. 10
MIT—Donna Coveney: p. 23; other: p. 28
NASA—p. 28
Science Photo Library—p. 8
George Steinmetz—pp. 6-7, 7, 8, 10, 11, 12, 14, 19, 20, 26
Texas A&M University—James Lyle: p. 12; Randall Davis: p. 18
UK Press—Antony Jones: p. 17
Visuals Unlimited, Inc.—Jeff J. Daly: pp. 12–13

Illustration credits:

Cover and all other illustrations—Justin Ray Thompson

Copyright © 2001
Kidsbooks, Inc.
230 Fifth Avenue
New York, NY 10001

Visit us at *www.kidsbooks.com*.
Volume discounts available for group purchases.

A Technology Q&A Book

Is That Robot Really My Doctor?

Written by
Rebecca L. Grambo

kidsbooks®
Incorporated

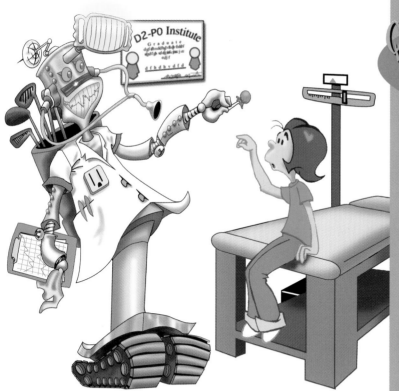

Q. How can a robot help me get hip?

A. RoboDoc *(below)* can't help you get hip, as in more cool. If you needed hip-replacement surgery, however, you would be happy to have RoboDoc on your surgery team! RoboDoc can drill a hole in exactly the right spot in a patient's thighbone, allowing surgeons to place the new hip implant in just the right spot and with just the right fit. Surgeons can also use a robotic system called HipNav. It projects the exact position of hip bones and joints onto a screen, so surgeons can see it—almost as clearly as if they were working on a skeleton!

Q. Is that robot really my doctor?

A. It could be someday. Robots already perform many kinds of hospital jobs, from delivering meals and medicines to sorting blood samples. Some robots control surgical tools in response to a doctor's voice commands, leaving the doctor's hands free to operate. New technology is allowing smaller and smaller robots to be built. Someday, tiny robots the size of bacteria may be sent cruising through a person's bloodstream. They could seek out and destroy harmful organisms, or remove fat deposits that threaten to block the flow of blood.

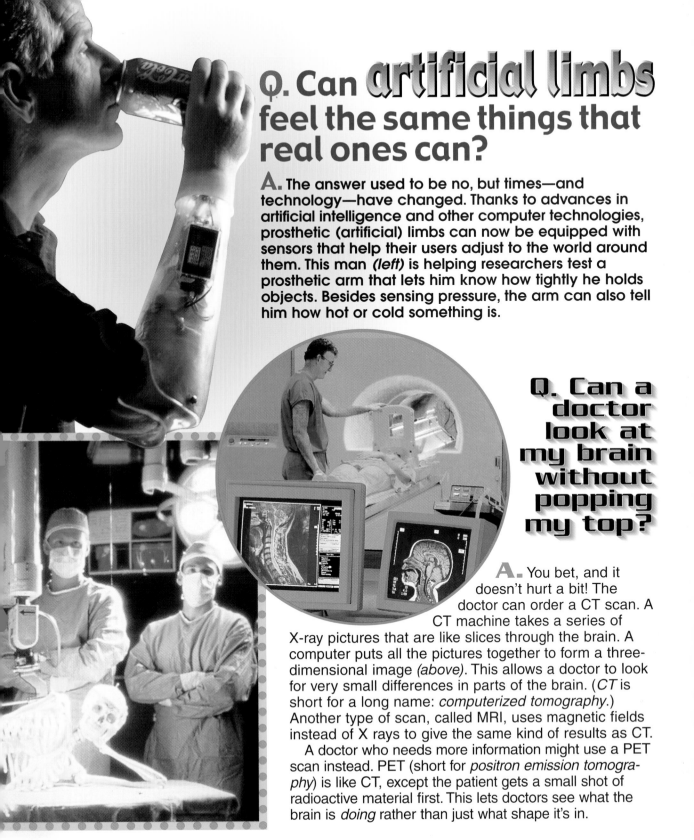

Q. Can artificial limbs feel the same things that real ones can?

A. The answer used to be no, but times—and technology—have changed. Thanks to advances in artificial intelligence and other computer technologies, prosthetic (artificial) limbs can now be equipped with sensors that help their users adjust to the world around them. This man *(left)* is helping researchers test a prosthetic arm that lets him know how tightly he holds objects. Besides sensing pressure, the arm can also tell him how hot or cold something is.

Q. Can a doctor look at my brain without popping my top?

A. You bet, and it doesn't hurt a bit! The doctor can order a CT scan. A CT machine takes a series of X-ray pictures that are like slices through the brain. A computer puts all the pictures together to form a three-dimensional image *(above)*. This allows a doctor to look for very small differences in parts of the brain. (*CT* is short for a long name: *computerized tomography*.) Another type of scan, called MRI, uses magnetic fields instead of X rays to give the same kind of results as CT.

A doctor who needs more information might use a PET scan instead. PET (short for *positron emission tomography*) is like CT, except the patient gets a small shot of radioactive material first. This lets doctors see what the brain is *doing* rather than just what shape it's in.

Q. Could a doctor ever walk through my heart?

A. Not really, but in the future, virtual-reality (VR) technology might let doctors *think* they were there. Computers could combine photographs of patients with their X rays or CAT scans to form 3-D VR images. A surgeon wearing a VR headset *(right)* could rehearse the surgery ahead of time. Zooming in for an inside close-up would let the surgeon feel as if he or she were inside the patient's body. Surgeons already can perform delicate operations—such as heart surgery—by using VR-type controls. The controls translate the surgeon's hand movements into instructions for a robot surgeon doing the actual work. A robot's movements are much more precise than a human's. Also, robots can operate through smaller cuts than human surgeons, speeding patients' recovery time.

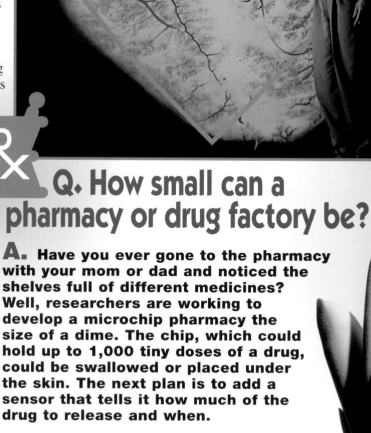

Q. How small can a pharmacy or drug factory be?

A. Have you ever gone to the pharmacy with your mom or dad and noticed the shelves full of different medicines? Well, researchers are working to develop a microchip pharmacy the size of a dime. The chip, which could hold up to 1,000 tiny doses of a drug, could be swallowed or placed under the skin. The next plan is to add a sensor that tells it how much of the drug to release and when.

Q. Can bacteria do a dentist's job?

A. No, but a new form of bacteria could mean less drilling and filling work for dentists. Bacteria—such as those in the petri dish below—are microscopic plants that live almost everywhere, including in our bodies. Many types of bacteria are harmless; others can cause us problems. Some scientists have been studying the bacteria that cause cavities. Using genetic engineering, they have come up with a new form of those bacteria—one that no longer makes the acid that harms teeth. After a dentist squirts this new bacteria on your teeth, they eventually replace their cavity-causing cousins, keeping decay away!

Q. What kind of liquid can we breathe like air?

A.
A liquid called perflubron. It does the job of carrying oxygen and carbon dioxide almost as well as air. Perflubron—a close relative of nonstick plastics—does not mix with water. In some illnesses, patients die because their lungs fill with watery fluids. Doctors are saving lives by using perflubron to fill the lungs and force out the harmful fluids. Babies born too early often have problems with fluid in their lungs; doctors hope that perflubron might be able to help them, too.

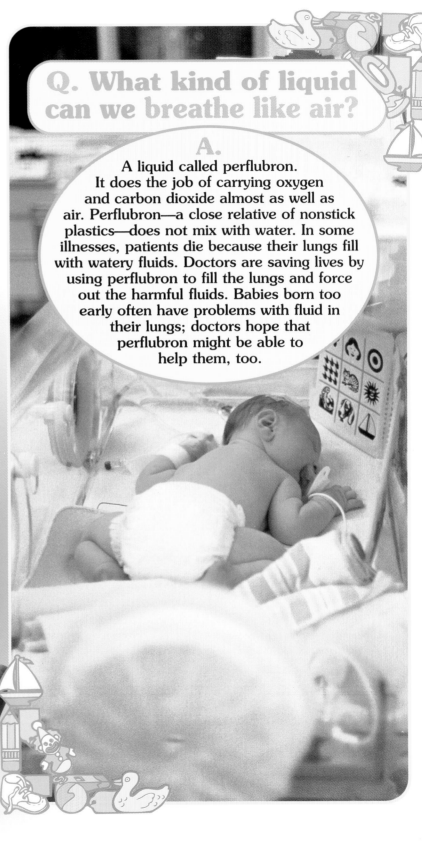

Q. What kind of insect plays hide-and-go-seek with gold?

A. Robotic ants programmed to hunt for food. Scientists working to improve artificial intelligence have come up with many different ways of teaching robots to perform various tasks. These tiny robots *(left)* are part of a robotic ant farm. Like regular ants, they have been programmed to perform many of the complex tasks that real ants perform—and, like real ants, to work together. These particular "ants" have been programmed to find food—in this case, gold foil—and take it back to their "nest."

Q. What kind of pen saves trees?

A. A new pen that contains a tiny computer able to read handwriting. The pen, called SmartQuill, may reduce our need for paper. When a person writes with this pen, sensors detect even the smallest hand motions. The pen's computer translates those motions into typed letters or words. This information can be read off the pen's screen, or sent to a printer or computer. SmartQuill doesn't need paper. It can read anything written on a horizontal or vertical surface—even if it is written in the air. You don't need to worry about other people misusing your "smart" pen, either: It recognizes its owner's signature, and won't work until *you* write it!

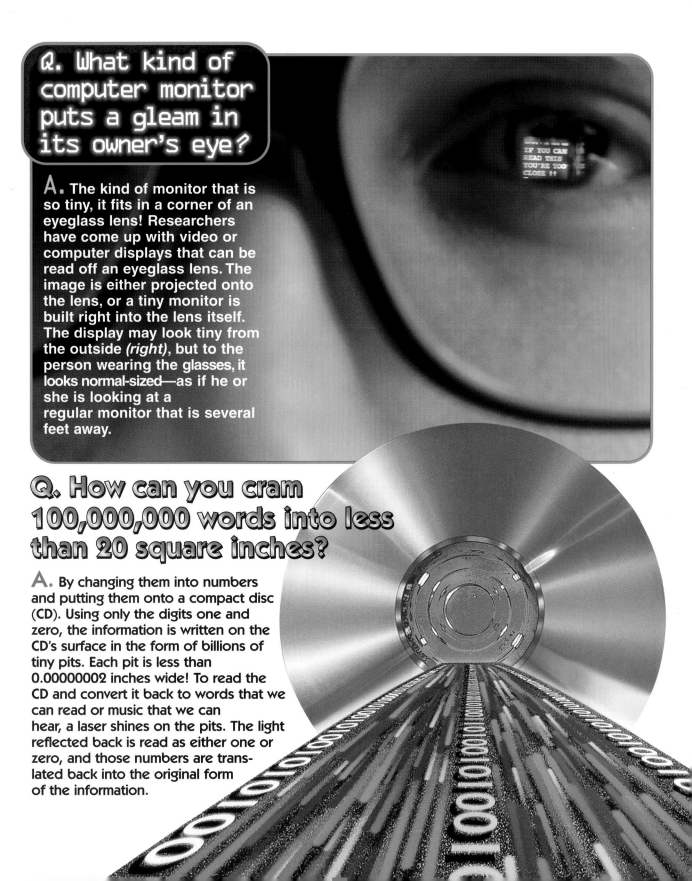

Q. What kind of computer monitor puts a gleam in its owner's eye?

A. The kind of monitor that is so tiny, it fits in a corner of an eyeglass lens! Researchers have come up with video or computer displays that can be read off an eyeglass lens. The image is either projected onto the lens, or a tiny monitor is built right into the lens itself. The display may look tiny from the outside *(right)*, but to the person wearing the glasses, it looks normal-sized—as if he or she is looking at a regular monitor that is several feet away.

IF YOU CAN
READ THIS
YOU'RE TOO
CLOSE !!

Q. How can you cram 100,000,000 words into less than 20 square inches?

A. By changing them into numbers and putting them onto a compact disc (CD). Using only the digits one and zero, the information is written on the CD's surface in the form of billions of tiny pits. Each pit is less than 0.00000002 inches wide! To read the CD and convert it back to words that we can read or music that we can hear, a laser shines on the pits. The light reflected back is read as either one or zero, and those numbers are trans-lated back into the original form of the information.

Q. Who will take care of my garden when I'm far away at school, work, or on vacation?

A. You, of course! "Telegarden" *(right)* lets gardeners tend living plants and flowers from remote locations. The Telegarden's computer can be hooked to the Internet, giving the gardener access from anywhere in the world. The Telegarden robot has monitors that show and tell gardeners how their plants are doing. It can also water and fertilize the plants according to instructions sent by the gardener. One thing that Telegarden *can't* do for you, though—at least not yet—is smell those flowers!

Q. What are those crunchy purple things in my lunch?

A. They could be carrots! A scientist in Texas has bred a carrot full of things that may help fight off cancer and slow down the effects of getting old. A side effect of these substances was changing the carrot's outer color from the familiar orange to a dark purplish-red *(left)*.

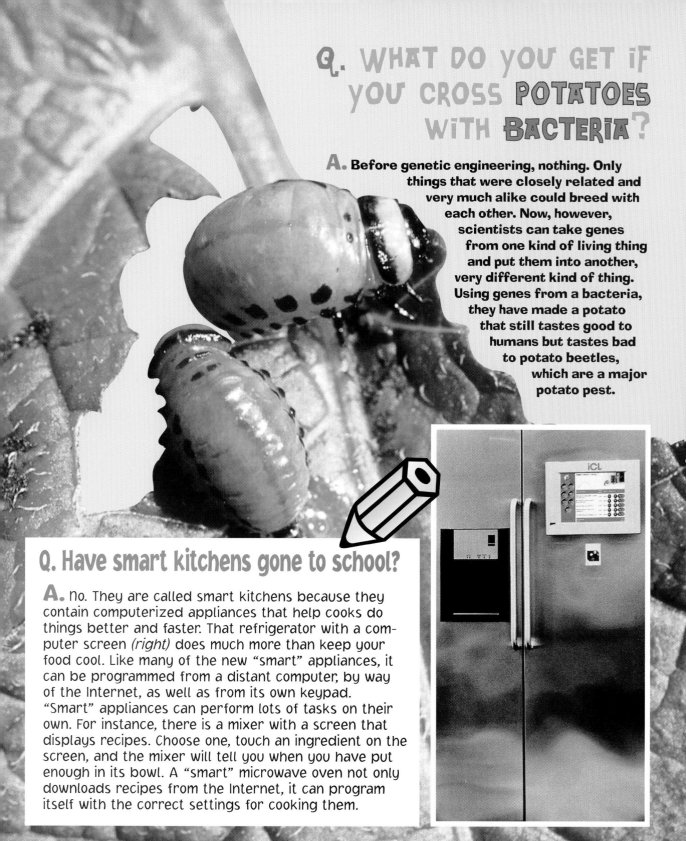

Q. WHAT DO YOU GET IF YOU CROSS POTATOES WITH BACTERIA?

A. Before genetic engineering, nothing. Only things that were closely related and very much alike could breed with each other. Now, however, scientists can take genes from one kind of living thing and put them into another, very different kind of thing. Using genes from a bacteria, they have made a potato that still tastes good to humans but tastes bad to potato beetles, which are a major potato pest.

Q. Have smart kitchens gone to school?

A. No. They are called smart kitchens because they contain computerized appliances that help cooks do things better and faster. That refrigerator with a computer screen *(right)* does much more than keep your food cool. Like many of the new "smart" appliances, it can be programmed from a distant computer, by way of the Internet, as well as from its own keypad. "Smart" appliances can perform lots of tasks on their own. For instance, there is a mixer with a screen that displays recipes. Choose one, touch an ingredient on the screen, and the mixer will tell you when you have put enough in its bowl. A "smart" microwave oven not only downloads recipes from the Internet, it can program itself with the correct settings for cooking them.

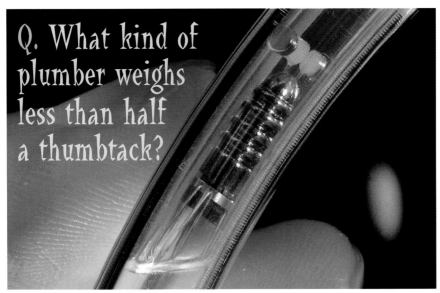

Q. What kind of plumber weighs less than half a thumbtack?

A. Japanese researchers have invented a tiny robot to find even the tiniest pipe leaks in places like power plants. These robots can crawl where there are lots of pipes jammed close together, or even crawl around in the very narrow spaces between pipes. Each of these robot workers is armed with a tiny camera and a transmitter that sends back information on what it finds.

Q. How can technology defeat stinky socks?

A. Scientists have come up with a new way to kill the microbes (germs) that cause the stink. A compound that contains chlorine atoms is applied to the cloth in a process sort of like the one that makes permanent-press clothes. The chlorine, which kills the stinky germs, gets used up after killing germs for a while but can be recharged by including bleach in every fourth or fifth wash. This new compound will be great for lots of things other than just socks, including sportswear, hospital bedding, and household sponges.

Q. How can a chicken help me clean up the drink I just spilled?

A. Chickens are not much help around the house—but their feathers can be! Scientists have found a way to make paper and plastic out of chicken feathers, which used to be considered garbage. Someday soon, the paper towels you use to clean up a mess, the insulation in your house, and even the dashboard of your car may all be a little "fowl"!

Q. How do they get that nonstick coating to stick to the pan?

A. It used to be pretty tricky: Manufacturers relied on force to jam the coating into tiny cavities in each pan's metal surface. This didn't work very well or last very long. Today, however, there is a better way: The molecules on the base of the nonstick coating are made differently from those on the surface. Bottom molecules have "chains" that poke out on the sides and stick to the metal, while top molecules are long and slithery, to keep those scrambled eggs from sticking to your frying pan.

Q. Why doesn't my new pet dog bark?

A. Maybe his batteries have run down! Robot dogs (*left*), which don't need to be walked or fed, are becoming very popular in some places. Some of these dogs use a special kind of computer programming called *artificial intelligence* to learn from their experiences. Over time, each robot dog behaves a little differently from the others, giving it something like its own personality. Even so, these robot toys still have a long way to go before they are as smart or as snuggly as a real puppy!

Q. What do fireworks and a professor in England have in common?

A. Both contain computer chips! The microchips placed in the fireworks are used to set them off. The chips can be programmed with special timing and safety instructions, making the fireworks safer and more predictable. The professor had surgery to place a tiny computer-controlled transmitter/receiver in his arm. It keeps track of his smallest movements and nerve impulses, and sends the information to a computer. This is the first time a human body has communicated directly to a computer! This kind of monitor could be a great help in many areas of medicine. Someday, it may allow us to operate a computer or drive a car by simply wiggling our fingers.

Q. Why do robots go to bowling alleys?

A. To bowl, of course! Bowling-ball manufacturers have used human test-bowlers for a long time. The test bowlers throw newly designed balls over and over again to see how they perform. But even the best professional bowlers don't always throw the ball the same way each time. So the ball manufacturers came up with Throbot. Weighing in at 1,600 pounds, Throbot is bigger and not as stylish as the humans it replaces, but it is much more consistent. Researchers can control the direction, speed, and release height of each throw, among other things.

Q. How did kangaroos help design a new kind of shoe?

A. Watching kangaroos hop helped a college student design "bionic boots." The student, Keahi Seymour (*right*), noticed that kangaroos bounce right along, even though they aren't all that strong. Stretchy tendons in their legs help absorb impact and hang on to the energy that is usually lost when a foot hits the ground. Seymour's bionic boots use high-powered springs and elastic devices to get the same effect: People wearing them get less tired and can take longer strides. Seymour hopes to market his bionic boots for hiking and other outdoor activities. Someday, they also may be helpful to people who have trouble walking.

Q. Why is that seal wearing a camcorder on its head?

A.
To help solve the Weddell riddle. Scientists have known for a long time that Weddell seals in Antarctica dive as deep as 600 feet below the water's surface to hunt. What scientists could not figure out—until now—was how and why the seals go down so far. Mounting a camcorder on a deep-diving seal *(above)*, along with monitors that track time and depth, has helped researchers finally discover where the seal goes and what it does there.

Q. How could seashells keep your car looking good?

A. Seashells, such as those made by the abalone, are very tough and resist scratches and dents. Don't you wish you had that for your car? Don't worry, you won't have to glue seashells to your car to protect it! Scientists have found a way to make an artificial seashell that is as strong as the real thing—and you can see through it! This material could be used to make scratchproof eyeglass lenses or nearly unbreakable windshields. It could even be sprayed onto the surface of cars, where it would harden into a shell that keeps those glossy paint jobs looking factory-fresh.

Q. Do cell phones watch the Weather Channel?

A. No, but in the future your cell phone might help you avoid dangerous weather. Scientists and government officials are looking at quick ways to get official warnings to people in danger. One of the possibilities is to set up a system in which cell phones let their owners know when a tornado, hurricane, or flood is approaching. Many people can already program their phones to give them weather alerts. Special receivers are available that automatically turn on radios and TVs when they detect a warning broadcast.

Q. WHY WOULD A COCKROACH CARRY A BACKPACK?

A. To help scientists study the natural electrical signals that control body movements in humans and other animals. Researchers at Tokyo University have equipped cockroach "biobots," like the one at right, with tiny computerized back-packs. The backpack sends signals to the roach's nervous system, telling the animal to walk, then records where it goes and how it moves.

Q. How do you get a TIGER out of a test tube?

A. There are very few tigers left in the world. Many of those that remain live in zoos that are far apart. In order to raise healthy baby tigers, it is important to get a good mix of genes from parent tigers—not just breed the tigers that happen to live closest together. Scientists can now combine frozen tiger sperm with eggs in a laboratory. Once a new tiger begins to develop, it is transplanted into a foster mother while it is still very, very tiny. This "test-tube" technology allows scientists to breed animals separated by great distances and raise more tigers than would happen in the wild.

Q. Could scientists put a computer inside my brain?

A. No, but Dr. Peter Fromherz *(below)* and other researchers are looking for ways to make it possible. The photo magnified on the screen behind Fromherz shows a rat brain cell combined with a computer chip. Special brain cells called *neurons* are a key working part of the brains of humans and other animals. Silicon chips are a key working part of the "brains" of computers. Fromherz is experimenting with growing rat neurons directly on computer chips. It's a long way from that to putting computer chips into human brains, but someday, who knows?

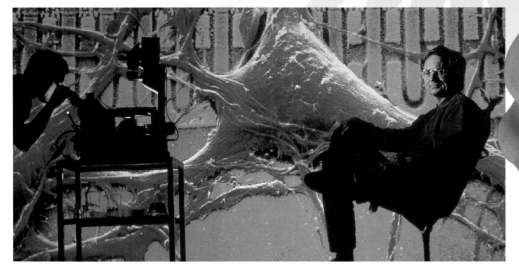

Q. Could a farmer ever grow a crop of toys?

A. Not exactly, but farmers might grow the raw material. Plastic made from petroleum (oil) is nearly indestructible, which makes it great for tough jobs. However, it also creates a big problem. Once the plastic gets thrown away it takes up a lot of space in landfills and garbage dumps. So scientists are experimenting with ways to create *plants* that can grow biodegradable plastic! (*Biodegradable* means that it breaks down into harmless substances.) The plants are a renewable resource, which means we won't run out of it, as we may with petroleum. The process is very expensive, and the plants produce only a small amount of plastic that isn't as tough as the other kind. However, scientists are working on ways to increase the harvest and produce a cheaper, tougher crop.

Q. What do you get when you cross a jellyfish with a potato?

A. A potato that tells you when it needs watering—by glowing! It is hard to guess how much water potatoes need, so farmers often overwater their crop. Hoping to fix that problem, scientists in Scotland put jellyfish protein—which causes fluorescence, or glowing—into potato cells. When a potato needs water, it produces an acid. That acid triggers the jellyfish protein, making the potato glow yellow! The glow is too dim for the human eye to see, but special monitors placed in a potato field can spot it. They send a signal that lets the farmer know the plants need watering. Only a few glowing plants are needed in each field.

Q. Can I get a drink from an atomic fountain?

A. No, but it can help you set your watch. The most accurate clocks in the world use the vibrations of atoms to keep time. Scientists chill atoms and observe them in a special chamber called an atomic fountain (above). Based on their observations, scientists can keep accurate time. Over 30 million years, an atomic fountain clock will not gain or lose more than one second!

Q. What kind of train doesn't touch the tracks?

A. A maglev—short for *magnetic-levitation*—train. Some maglev trains have magnets on board that push away from magnets in the tracks, causing the train to levitate (float) above the track. Others have winglike flaps that wrap around, but don't touch, a T-shaped guideway. This type of maglev train has magnets underneath that are attracted to those in the track.

Some maglevs run on wheels until they reach a certain speed, then they begin to float. Most are designed to travel at about 310 miles per hour, which is two to three times faster than ordinary trains. Maglevs are quieter and safer than trains that run on ordinary tracks.

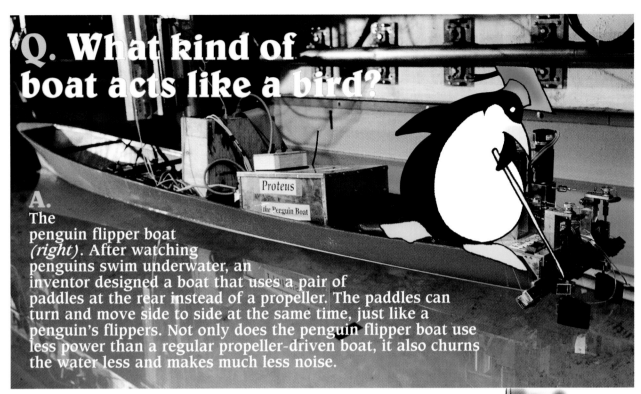

Q. What kind of boat acts like a bird?

A. The penguin flipper boat *(right)*. After watching penguins swim underwater, an inventor designed a boat that uses a pair of paddles at the rear instead of a propeller. The paddles can turn and move side to side at the same time, just like a penguin's flippers. Not only does the penguin flipper boat use less power than a regular propeller-driven boat, it also churns the water less and makes much less noise.

Q. Does it take a magician to make a building float in the air?

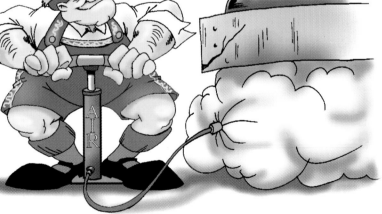

A. Not anymore. In Berlin, Germany, engineers needed to move Emperor's Hall, a famous building, to a new location. How do you get a two-story, 1,300-ton building to travel 246 feet around a corner? Engineers placed eight huge jacks under carefully chosen parts of the building. Compressed air was pumped in under the jacks to create a cushion. Next, using a computer to control the whole system, the jacks lifted the building off its foundation and raised it almost eight feet! Then—like the puck in an air-hockey game—Emperor's Hall glided on a cushion of air to its new home.

Q. What happened soon after several hundred people in Virginia received an 84-second phone call?

A. Police found an elderly man who had become lost. The man needed regular medication, so the police used a computer system that called people living near where the man went missing and played a message about him. Within three hours, a neighbor who had heard the message on his answering machine gave police information that helped them find the lost man. This type of system is also useful for alerting people in specific areas of local emergencies, such as a chemical-plant fire or an accident at a nuclear-power plant.

Q. When would I be really happy to see a dog with a camera on its head?

A. If you were trapped in a collapsed building after an earthquake. It is hard to find survivors among the rubble left by an earthquake. Dogs have long been used to help search-and-rescue workers, but new technology can make them even more helpful. Dogs can be equipped with infrared cameras that send pictures to rescue workers. The pictures show heat patterns that reveal the location of living bodies. A trapped person found by a dog can use a microphone and speaker in the dog's collar to talk with rescuers.

24

Q. Can a satellite tell me how to get home?

A. Yes—if it is part of the global positioning system (GPS). Several GPS satellites orbit Earth. When a person with a GPS receiver *(right)* stands out in the open and turns it on, it takes signals from satellites that are within range. It then calculates where on Earth the user is, to within about 50 yards! The user can find this location on a map, compare it to where he or she wants to be, then head in the right direction. GPS receivers are especially useful in places where everything looks the same for miles, such as deserts or oceans.

Q. What can a robot and a huge lake you can't see tell us about life in outer space?

A. Lake Vostok is a fresh-water lake in Antarctica that is as big as Lake Ontario. It lies near the South Pole, under ice that is 2.5 miles thick. Scientists are working on a special robot, called a cryobot, designed to melt its way down through the ice to reach the lake. The cryobot, which they hope to start using in December 2001, will send off a smaller hydrobot *(right)* to swim in the lake and report back to the cryobot what it finds. The water in Lake Vostok has not been in contact with Earth's surface for perhaps a million years. If life is found there, it might give scientists ideas about what life-forms might be able to exist in the ice oceans of Europa, one of Jupiter's moons.

Q. WHO NEVER MINDS STANDING IN THE MIDDLE OF THE HIGHWAY, NO MATTER HOW MANY TIMES HE IS HIT BY CARS?

A. Anzen Taro, also known as Safety Sam. (*Anzen* is Japanese for "safety"; *Taro* is a common Japanese first name.) Anzen Taro *(below)* is a highway-construction warning robot tough enough to withstand the heaviest traffic, no matter what the hour or the weather. The flagmen and women who steer traffic clear of highway construction sites have a dangerous job, especially at night. Anzen Taro is a real lifesaver: Each year, five to ten of these robots are struck by cars or trucks—accidents that would have killed or seriously wounded a human traffic guide.

Q. What do bulletproof vests and happy mountain-bike riders have in common?

A. Kevlar. Lightweight Kevlar fibers are five times stronger than steel! They are woven into material that is made into vests and helmets worn by soldiers and police. Kevlar fabric is strong enough to stop a bullet or bomb fragment. However, objects with thin, sharp points can get between the threads of the fabric and cause injury. To solve this problem, scientists have come up with a liquid form of Kevlar. It can seal those gaps, making protective clothing and helmets stabproof as well as bulletproof. A bike company has used this form of Kevlar to protect mountain-bike tires from thorns, pieces of metal, and broken glass.

Q. How could my hair put me in jail?

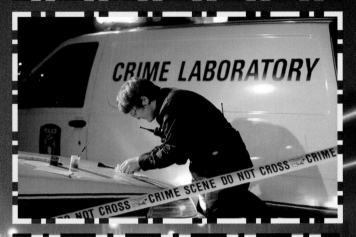

A. If police find a strand of hair at the scene of a crime, they can use it to learn a lot about the person it came from, including age and whether that person is male or female. They can prove whose head that hair came from by studying the hair's DNA. DNA (deoxyribonucleic acid) is the substance in our genes that makes each of us unique. Recently developed tests allow scientists to get DNA from hair, flakes of skin, or even the saliva in used chewing gum. DNA information from crime-scene material can then be compared with that of a suspect to see if it matches.

Q. How can you make an airplane INVISIBLE?

A. We can't really, but the B-2 "stealth" bomber comes close. Even with a 172-foot wingspan, the B-2 can be hard to find. The plane's body is built with materials that trap radar waves inside. Its surface is designed with very few right angles or flat areas, which reflect radar. These features make the B-2 appear to be the same size as a bird on a radar screen—almost as good as being invisible. The B-2's engines are designed to be extra quiet, making it hard to hear. The engine exhaust is cooled before it leaves the plane, leaving no target for heat-seeking missiles. When you finally do catch a glimpse of the B-2, its shape makes it hard to tell which is the front and which is the back!

Q. How small can a rocket be?

A. Tiny—the microrocket at left is sitting on a dime! An even smaller microrocket would fit on the period at the end of this sentence—or on a microchip. A microchip's layers have tiny pockets in them, which scientists fill with tiny amounts of fuel. When that fuel is given a jolt of electricity, it explodes. This micro-explosion produces only a very small amount of thrust, but when millions of miniature rocket pockets are fired—all at once or one right after the other—it creates enough thrust to steer one of the new, very small satellites. How small are these satellites? The size of a deck of playing cards!

Q. What kind of boat uses a solar sail?

A. Solar sails are not found on boats, but they may be a great power source for spacecraft. A solar sail *(left)* is made of a lightweight, highly reflective plastic. Light from the sun strikes the sail's surface, giving a very tiny push. In space, that can be enough to propel a spacecraft. The spacecraft's orbit can be adjusted by tilting the sail. Solar sails don't provide the speed of rockets, but they are much cheaper, simpler, and safer.

Q. What kind of airplane skips?

A. The new HyperSoar aircraft will skip along the top of Earth's atmosphere like a stone skipping across the water, hitting the atmosphere every 1,200 miles or so. It will use a new kind of engine, called the scramjet, that was designed at NASA. The HyperSoar will be able to fly 10 times faster than the speed of sound. It now takes 10 hours to fly from San Francisco to Tokyo. The HyperSoar will cover the same distance in an hour and a half! It will fly high in the sky—above 100,000 feet.

Q. Can a nose keep me from getting an upset stomach?

A. Electronic noses are sensitive air-sampling machines. They compare chemicals in the air with patterns stored in their memory. (The nose at right is "smelling" coffee beans.) One of the places where electronic noses may be helpful in the future is in space. Scientists at NASA hope that electronic noses aboard the Space Shuttle and other aircraft will be able to detect odors. The noses could alert the crew to gas leaks or any changes in air quality in the cabin that could make them sick.

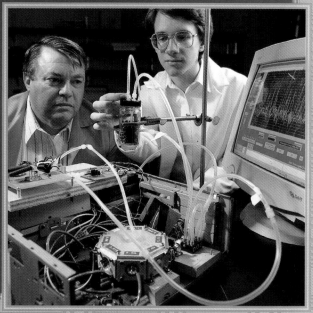

Glossary

Atmosphere: Layers of air and other gases that surround Earth.

Atom: The smallest particle of any substance. (Atoms connected together form molecules.)

Bacteria: Simple, microscopic plants.

CT scan: A special scan that allows doctors to see inside your body. (*CT* stands for computerized tomography.)

DNA: The substance that tells each of our cells how to behave. (*DNA* stands for deoxyribonucleic acid.)

Genetic engineering: The practice of changing the behavior of a cell by altering its genes.

Infrared camera: A camera that detects and records heat.

Kevlar: A very strong and durable substance.

Magnetic levitation: When magnets are used to lift or move something.

Microchip: A tiny electronic device that can store lots of information.

Molecule: The smallest complete unit of any substance. (Molecules are made up of atoms.)

MRI: A special scan that uses magnets to allow doctors to see inside your body. (*MRI* stands for magnetic resonance imaging.)

Neuron: A type of brain cell.

PET scan: A special scan that allows doctors to see electrical activity in your brain. (*PET* stands for positron emission tomography.)

Radar: A device that uses radio waves to locate objects.

Robot: A machine that does tasks otherwise performed by humans.

Virtual reality: A computer-generated environment within which people can interact.